W9-ABA-170

ADDITION

2 + 2 = 4

Paul Challen

Crabtree Publishing Company

www.crabtreebooks.com

Author: Paul Challen
Coordinating editor: Chester Fisher
Series editor: Penny Dowdy
Editor: Reagan Miller
Proofreader: Ellen Rodger
Editorial director: Kathy Middleton
Production coordinator: Margaret Amy Salter
Prepress technician: Margaret Amy Salter
Cover design: Samara Parent
Logo design: Samantha Crabtree
Project manager: Kumar Kunal (Q2AMEDIA)
Art direction: Dibakar Acharjee (Q2AMEDIA)
Design: Shruti Aggarwal (Q2AMEDIA)
Photo research: Poulomi Basu (Q2AMEDIA)

Photographs:
Corbis: Jon Feingersh: p. 15 (top left), 23 (top);
    Patrik Giardino: p. 13 (top); Stephanie Weiler:
    p. 13 (bottom)
Getty Images: Bob Thomas: p. 15 (top right), 23 (bottom)
Istockphoto: Francesco Rossetti p. 4 (bottom right), p. 7 (right)
Jupiter Images: Comstock Images: front cover (center)
Masterfile: p. 11, 20 (bottom right)
Photolibrary: Tim Macpherson: p. 20 (bottom left)
Q2AMedia Art Bank: p. 5, 9, 17, 18, 19, 21
Shutterstock: Alekcey: front cover (bottom right);
    Daniel Goodchild: p. 5; Ramon Grosso Dolarea:
    p. 17; Edyta Pawlowska: p. 9; Alessio Ponti:
    p. 4 (bottom left), p. 7 (left), 9; MatkaWariatka: p. 1

Library and Archives Canada Cataloguing in Publication

Challen, Paul, 1967-
    Addition / Paul Challen.

(My path to math)
Includes index.
ISBN 978-0-7787-4345-3 (bound).--ISBN 978-0-7787-4363-7 (pbk.)

    1. Addition--Juvenile literature. I. Title. II. Series: My path to math

QA115.C43 2009   j513.2'11   C2009-903577-4

Library of Congress Cataloging-in-Publication Data

Challen, Paul C. (Paul Clarence), 1967-
   Addition / Paul Challen.
      p. cm. -- (My path to math)
   Includes index.
   ISBN 978-0-7787-4345-3 (reinforced lib. bdg. : alk. paper)
   -- ISBN 978-0-7787-4363-7 (pbk. : alk. paper)
   1. Addition--Juvenile literature. I. Title.
   QA115.C43 2010
   513.2'11--dc22
                                                    2009022911

Crabtree Publishing Company

www.crabtreebooks.com   1-800-387-7650

Published in Canada
Crabtree Publishing
616 Welland Ave.
St. Catharines, ON
L2M 5V6

Published in the United States
Crabtree Publishing
PMB16A
350 Fifth Ave., Suite 3308
New York, NY 10118

Published in the United Kingdom
Crabtree Publishing
Lorna House, Suite 3.03, Lorna Road
Hove, East Sussex, UK
BN3 3EL

Published in Australia
Crabtree Publishing
386 Mt. Alexander Rd.
Ascot Vale (Melbourne)
VIC 3032

Contents

How Many Balls?

Kelly is at the soccer field. She cannot wait to play! Maggie is her coach.

Last week, the team used 6 balls. Today, Maggie has 3 new balls. Kelly wonders how many balls the team has now. Kelly's friend Henry plays on the team, too. Henry knows how to figure out how many balls they have all together.

Kelly and Henry talk to Coach Maggie.

Put It All Together

Henry will use **addition** to find the total number of soccer balls. This means he will find the **sum**. The sum is the answer to an addition problem. When Henry **adds**, he uses special words and symbols.

Words like, "all together" tell Henry to add. Some other addition words are:

Addition Words	Example
all together	How many is 6 balls and 3 balls **all together**?
in all	How many balls **in all**?
total	What is the **total** number of balls?
add	**Add** 6 and 3.
plus	What is 6 **plus** 3?

Fact Box

A **number line** can help Henry and Kelly add numbers.

Addition has a **symbol**. We call it a **plus sign**. It looks like this: +. The sum has a symbol, too. We call it an **equal sign**. It looks like this: =.

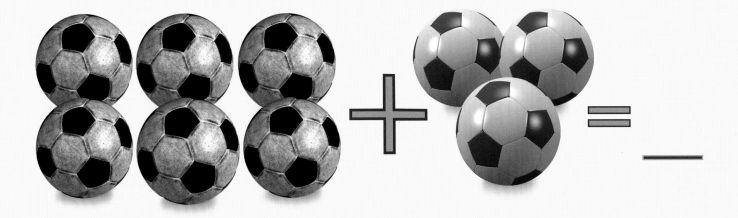

Henry shows Kelly how to solve this addition problem using a number line.

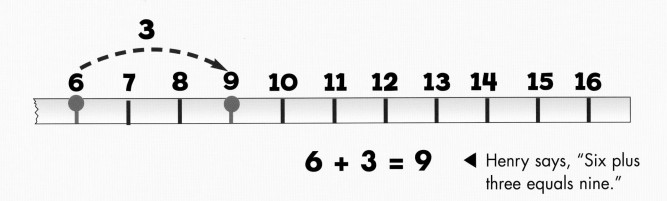

6 + 3 = 9   ◀ Henry says, "Six plus three equals nine."

Zero Problems

Henry shows Kelly the easiest addition problem. He will add 0 to a number. The sum of 0 and a number is just the number you added. So 0 + 2 = 2, and 0 + 200 = 200!

Henry shows Kelly his 2 shoes. If he adds 0 shoes, he will still have 2 of them. Henry does not have any extra feet after all!

Zero problems 2 + 0 = 2

Kelly says, "I know 2 plus 0 equals 2."

One More!

Henry sees 4 players standing together. Soon, 1 more player walks over to join the team. How many players in all?

Henry tells Kelly to start with 4 players. To add 1, she names the next number. The next number is 5. So 4 plus 1 equals 5! There are 5 players in all.

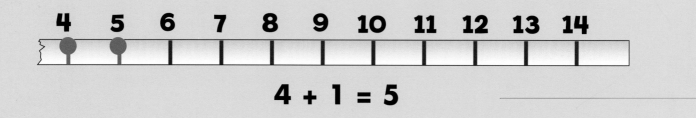

4 + 1 = 5

Activity Box

What is the highest number you can think of? What is the sum when you add 1?

By adding 1, Kelly found
that 4 plus 1 equals 5.

Just Count It!

Kelly wants to learn other ways to do addition. Henry shows her how to add by counting up. He points to a team of 5 girls. He will add the team of 4 boys. He starts at the larger number. Then he counts up by the second number.

Henry adds 5 girls plus 4 boys on paper.

5 + 4

Start at 5. Count up 4 with Henry to find the answer: 6, 7, 8, 9.

5 + 4 = 9

So 5 girls plus 4 boys equals 9 players!

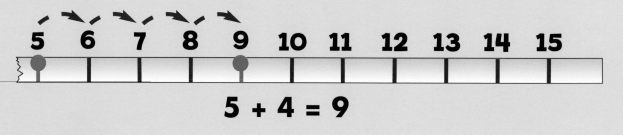

Fact Box

It does not matter what order you add numbers in. That means that 5 + 4 = 9, and 4 + 5 = 9 too!

◄ Five girls play on a team.

◄ Four more players join in.

Doubling Up

Maggie knows how to add the same numbers together. She calls these numbers **doubles**. She teaches Kelly and Henry to add doubles.

To add doubles, Maggie **skip-counts**. So to add 2+2, Maggie starts with 2 and skip-counts by 2. The sum equals 4.

2 + 2 = 4

To add 3 + 3, Maggie starts with 3 and skip-counts by 3. The sum equals 6.

3 + 3 = 6

4 + 4 = 8

5 + 5 = 10

Activity Box

What doubles do you see around you? How many tires on a bicycle? How many legs does a dog have?

◀ Four plus four means double the players!

| 1 | 2 | 3 | 4 | 5 | 6 | 7 | 8 | 9 | 10 | 11 |

1 + 1 = 2

| 2 | 3 | 4 | 5 | 6 | 7 | 8 | 9 | 10 | 11 | 12 |

2 + 2 = 4

| 3 | 4 | 5 | 6 | 7 | 8 | 9 | 10 | 11 | 12 | 13 |

3 + 3 = 6

| 4 | 5 | 6 | 7 | 8 | 9 | 10 | 11 | 12 | 13 | 14 |

4 + 4 = 8

| 5 | 6 | 7 | 8 | 9 | 10 | 11 | 12 | 13 | 14 | 15 |

5 + 5 = 10

A Little More

Henry tells Kelly that they can use adding doubles to solve other problems. Henry says they can use doubles to add two numbers that are close to doubles.

Henry writes a problem.
3 + 4

He says that 3 + 4 is very close to the double 3 + 3. It is just 1 more.
3 + 3 = 6

So 3 + 4 = 7

Kelly has an idea. She shows
Henry how to use another double.
4 + 4

She looks back at the 3 + 4 that Henry wrote.
Kelly says that 3 + 4 is very close to the
double 4 + 4. It is just 1 less.
4 + 4 = 8

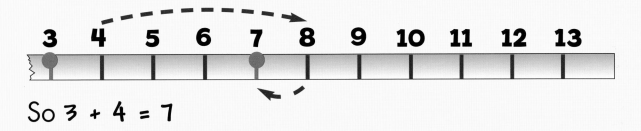

So 3 + 4 = 7

Henry explains how
to add numbers that
are close to doubles.

Adding It Up

Maggie shows the kids another way to add. She draws a chart to show them the number pairs that add up to ten:

These numbers go up.		These numbers go down.	
1	+	9	=10
2	+	8	=10
3	+	7	=10
4	+	6	=10
5	+	5	=10

Kelly remembers that she can add in any order. So,

These numbers go down.		These numbers go up.	
9	+	1	=10
8	+	2	=10
7	+	3	=10
6	+	4	=10
5	+	5	=10

Maggie explains that making a group of ten helps solve other addition problems, too. Think about 7 + 5.

Maggie knows that 7 + 3 = 10. She also knows that 5 is 2 more than 3. This means that 7 + 5 is 2 more than 7 + 3. So 7 + 5 = 12.

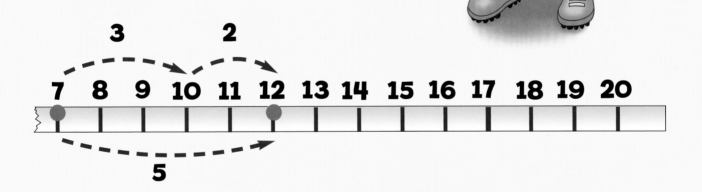

Activity Box

How would you solve the addition problem 9 + 9 by making a 10?

How Many Ways?

Henry and Kelly learned many ways to add. Maggie asks them to look around the field.

Henry and Kelly see two groups of players. They are wearing different color uniforms. There are 5 players wearing red uniforms, and 6 players wearing white uniforms. Maggie asks, "How many different ways can you add the people on the field? Use what you learned today."

◀ These 5 players are wearing red uniforms.

▶ These 6 players are wearing white uniforms.

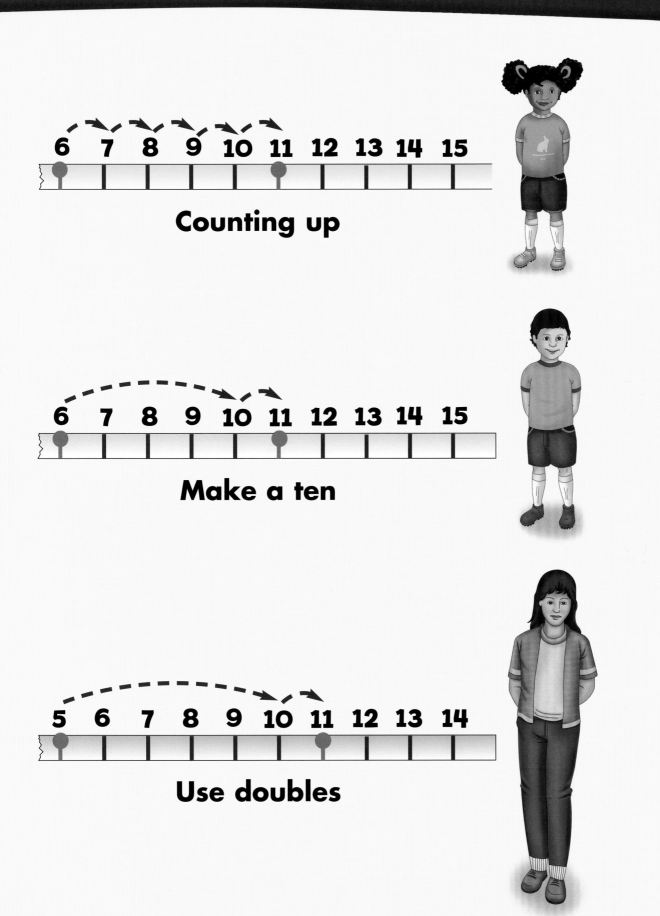

Counting up

Make a ten

Use doubles

Glossary

add To combine two or more numbers

addition Combining two or more amounts

doubles An addition problem with two of the same numbers

equal sign =

number line

| 0 | 1 | 2 | 3 | 4 | 5 | 6 | 7 | 8 | 9 | 10 |

plus sign +

skip-counting The pattern of counting by a number

sum The answer to an addition problem

symbol Something that stands for something else